Economic Leadership Solution

The Dawn Of The Age Of Enlightenment

Steve Alexander

http://crmediaonline.com

ISBN: **0615499856**
ISBN-13: **978-0615499857**

DEDICATION

I would like to dedicate this book to some of the greatest souls to have lived on planet earth,

Jesus the Christ, Mahatma Gandhi, Buddha, Moses, Father Abraham, Mohammed the Prophet, Sister Teresa, Dr. King, Confucius, Malcolm X, César Chavez, Abraham Lincoln, Nelson Mandela, Harriet Tubman, Frederick Douglas, Paul the Evangelist, Peter the Apostle, William Wilburforce, and all other spirit beings, who sought justice, righteousness, peace, and love between brothers and sisters all over the family of nations

I also want to dedicate and give thanks to my prayer partners, Angela my sister in Christ, who is also my beloved wife, and my best friend, my daughter Kisha, My sons Hasheem, Akeem, Rashad, my grandchildren Gregg, Erica, Mary, Nehemiah, and Cherish, my sister in Christ, Nadine Herrera, and the Frederick Church of Christ. Thank you guys for so many inspired prayers

Contents

AUTHOR'S NOTE

God has impressed upon me that I am the "Weeping Watchman."
My call is to lead the African-American community out of the deep
pit despair and destructive behaviors that we find ourselves in.
Having been raised in the segregated south, and having taken
advantage of educational opportunities, I am in the blessed position
of being able to share of my own struggles while boasting in God of
the great things He has done.

Together, as people of God, we are stronger than when we are
divided. Together we can rebuild our blighted inner cities and bring
prosperity to forgotten neighborhoods.

CHAPTER ONE

The Sacredness of Money

Economic Leadership Solution, or ELS, is a 21st century entity that believes that when a company is enriched by a community, that company's moral obligation is to enrich the community that has enriched it. An old reliable saying is that you reap what you sow, or what our grandparents told us as little children is "what goes around comes around." So if I want to thrive as an enterprise then I must walk in a symbiotic relationship (a relationship that is equally beneficial) with the community that has enriched my enterprise.

We must not look to short term gains or profits, which only benefits the enterprise and leaves the community short changed and devastated at its economic foundation. When this policy of greed and shortsightedness becomes epidemic in our economic policies, that flow down from Wall Street to main street, it lacks principal centered leadership and borders on economic treason.

So we the people of main street must take back power that is rendered through our constitution; we the people, of the people, by the people and for the people. This power is not found in government. Our government is in gridlock for many reasons.

I am not writing this introduction as a policy document, so I won't go into the internal dialog of why our government is failing us, it just is. Economic Leadership Solution (ELS) is the vehicle that we return power to the people simply by educating the masses about the sacredness of how we spend our money.

How we spend our money is the most powerful expression of our destiny. We who witness the stranglehold of segregation with all of its power of destruction to the African American people in the physical realm and the destruction of the White American in the spiritual realm. God said "No Slanderer Could Enter Heaven" and when one sees themselves as a superior to another creation that is made in the image of God, then that person has become a slanderer. God says, "If you cannot love your brother whom you can see, how can you love Him who you cannot see."

I wanted to explain how segregation had a stranglehold on all segments of our society as Dr. King so eloquently expressed. But back to the power and the sacredness of how we spend our sacred dollar, when Rosa Parks decided to stop paying for her own denigration through Dr. King's bus boycott, the black community found that the African people in America were enriching the bottom line profit of their oppressor. The white community found that they loved our money more than their slanderous false superiority complexes.

The sacredness of money goes back to the very foundation of our nation. Taxation without representation was the rallying cry at the Boston Tea Party. It is amazing the same curse that the British put upon America, America has now put upon the Africans in America, that have fought in every war from the revolutionary (the first to fall was a black man by the name of Crispus Attucks) to the Iraqi war. Africans in America have shed our blood for our nation, helping to build this nation on our backs through brutal slavery.

Following slavery there was another 100 years of unrepentant discrimination, where the Jim Crow laws sanctioned terror in the African American communities through lynching, blowing children up in churches, and educationally and economically crippling millions of people. This threw generations into despair and hopelessness because they had been systematically kept away from the sacred river of cash flow.

The Dawn of The Age of Enlightenment

Money is a terrible master but it is a great servant. You may say to call money sacred is blasphemous, but I say to you, go into any church on Sunday and you will find one of the acts of worship is the giving of money. This makes it sacred if it is a mandatory part of worship. So as long as I speak of money, I will speak of its sacredness and its power. We have spoken of two instances where money has been significant in our evolution as a nation. I will speak of a third instance, the development of unions.

Many tears went into building strong unions. You may ask why? I will tell you why, for that mighty dollar. All throughout American history the sacred dollar has reigned supreme.

We must change our attitude about this living entity. Though it seems inanimate, not biologically alive, it is like words, music or a beautiful painting. It moves us as much, if not more than any living biological entity. It moves nations to war, it dissolves marital relationships (for it is the number one cause of divorce), it moves people to kill for insurance policies, it causes people to denigrate their own bodies through prostitution. It moves young men to sell drugs and poison their own communities. It has no respect of class or race when it is being used in a profane orgy of greed.

Money is a terrible master, but a wonderful servant. Giving money in church is an act of worship, sustaining the church through evangelizing and outreach. Paying

Economic Leadership Solution

bills to sustain the sanctuary, reaching out to the poor for their needs, reaching out to the afflicted, to visit and bring good news to the oppressed, to clothe the naked and to visit and bring a new mind to the prisoners of our great nation, money can be used in Holy ways. Sacred money built our great learning institutions on the lower and higher end. It sustains homes and governments. It is likened to the blood in our physical bodies which is the very foundation of life. As blood is to the body, so is sacred money to our communities. When we have no viable commerce in the African American communities it leads to decay and destruction.

Because we lack the governmental or spiritual wisdom to rebuild our inner cities, we lose to bloodshed more African American boys everyday accumulative than we lose in the Iraq war. We lose 200 a year in Washington D C, over 300 a year in Philly and so on because we lack vision in how to rectify these problems. That is where Economic Leadership Solutions time has surely come. We will turn money from a terrible master to a wonderful servant. We will bring commerce into the inner cities by how we spend our money.

CHAPTER 2

Mind Of The Weeping Watchmen

The founder of the ELS journey began upon this physical realm on January 4, 1956. My spiritual name is "The weeping watchman." Like the prophet Ezekiel we are charged to be watchman over the souls of the family of nations. Man's condition makes me weep and cry out for a new mind; a mind of love and brotherhood unto all nations of men.

On that day in 1956, there were unheeded screams. My mother was dying. A midwife was set to deliver me through the birth canal, not knowing that my mother could only give birth through cesarean section. Those around her thought these desperate cries were from her birth pains, however they would become death pains if someone didn't act in a hurry. She calmed herself enough to make a quiet plea to my father that if he didn't get her a doctor she was going to die. The doctor arrived in time to save us both! I believe that was the first attack from the spirit world to stop me from my destiny to be a king. That may sound arrogant at first glance, but a king from a spiritual perspective is not one who is to be served but one who becomes a master servant in his community and then on to the community of nations.

We come from one man and one woman, Adam and Eve. Scientists have traced the DNA strand back to one woman and one man. I lived through that first attack but there would be many more. Some of these attacks were self-inflicted through drug use. Some came from outside forces like accidents, or being held at gunpoint in a robbery.

As I have grown in age and maturity, my understanding of the coexisting spiritual and physical worlds has grown as well. One must understand that we are three dimensional beings; body mind and soul. Our body is the physical house where our souls reside. It needs to breathe, eat and experience the five senses: sight, touch, smell, hearing, and taste. Through these senses we experience the world.

We lust or long after things we see. We are moved to the depth of our being. From a song or from the touch of our lips in an affectionate kiss from someone we love. By our touch, through sex we created life. We can smell a certain smell and it will transport us back to another time and place. We have a brain that computes faster than that of a computer. Our brain controls all of our body's voluntary and involuntary functions.

It is for this reason that when someone is pronounced brain dead they cut off the machines that keep the body functioning. Without the brain functioning the body is useless. There is an old saying, "Kill the head and the body will die".

Our skin is second to function next to the brain. Remember through touching of the skin we create life. I read a book "Magical Child" by Joseph Pearce some 30 years or more ago. It spoke about the importance of touching. There was an experiment by some doctors in the 15th century on some newborn babies. Some were held and stroked and were showered with much love and affection. They grew and developed exceptionally well. The other set of babies were given adequate nutrition to survive, but they were not held and cuddled and were not shown affection. Each child in the second group died. The conclusion drawn was that it is not material things that bring sufficiency to our survival, but it is tactile feedback.

It is love and affection that causes us to develop to our maximum potential. Even in the animal kingdom, we see animals licking their offspring in certain areas to start bodily functions. For example: a dog licking her puppies' genital areas to start the urination process. We too as the family of nations must begin to stimulate each other. We must learn to cuddle each other's children.

Economic Leadership Solution

We must see ourselves as a collective that is divided into individuals. Like the five fingers on each hand are individual, but yet they are connected collectively to the hand; with one purpose to serve the body. We as the family of nations are individuals by nations, but collectively are of the same earth. The earth is individually one planet, yet serves its purpose as one planet in our collective solar system. As surely as those children needed to be touched and loved to survive, we too as the family of nations need to touch each other through economic leadership solutions. Not to mention the heart, the lungs, the kidneys, the eyes, the ears, our respiratory and circulatory and digestive systems, we are so wonderfully made.

All human kind is 99.9% the same; built by a master builder. How can we talk about the great mural of King David without talking about Michael Angelo? How can we talk about Picasso's great works of arts without talking about him? How can we talk about the human experience without talking about the creator of our realities?

We have talked about the wonders of the body. Let us talk about the mind. It connects the physical and the spirit worlds together into one god-like entity. It is somewhat like a computer, as it gathers and holds memory of our human experiences. It is a database of individual and collective memory from the human experience, like the computer garbage in, garbage out.

The Dawn of The Age of Enlightenment

That is why social and environmental experiences have such a large impact on who we will become. The mind is either a slave to the physical dimension or a slave to the spiritual dimension. The spiritual part of us is our soul. That is why we are god-like in our essence; we are eternal beings by nature. We do not die, we transcend from the physical world to the spirit world when we lay our mortal bodies down to death.

I like to call them our earth suits, like the suits astronauts need to wear to survive in space. We need to enclose our eternal selves in these earth suits to have the human experience; we are spirit beings having the human experience.

One might ask what the human experience is. It is experiencing a mother's love, a father's strength, a brother's leadership, a sister's compassion, a friend's loyalty, puppy love, education, athletic competition, a wife's devotion and passion, her oneness of purpose with you in raising a family, your soul mate who walk through this turbulent human experience side by side with you, enduring all of life storms together. The human experience is to parent children that have been placed in your care by our creator; to nourish them; to teach them to live at the height of the human experience. It is not to teach false doctrines to them that leads to their spiritual death, but to be living examples, teaching that all men and women are created equal, with inalienable rights, to choose their own spiritual and physical destinies.

Further, one should teach their children that respecting all cultures does not intrude upon the individual human rights. These inalienable rights must never be denied by the use of weapons or psychological coercion. Children should be taught to never look down on any race or to never look down on any class of people, instilling in them the truth that we all derive from one man (it tells us in the book of life in Acts chapter 17:26).

From one man came every nation of men choosing the exact time and place of their dwelling, teaching that our creators built this world and everything in it so that we would seek Him with all our hearts, and we truly would find him. When we find him, we find love for each other. We find brotherhood with each other, knowing that the DNA strand cannot lie, and the DNA strand verifies that all men can be traced back to one woman. We Christians can call her Eve.

Our children must be taught that their mother and our mothers came from the same blood. We are the family of man. If we teach our children these eternal truths then we will build a new world, one where brothers and sisters want the best for each other knowing that if I plant the best for you and your family, I will reap in return what I have sown. So if I want to be loved and I want my family to be loved, then I must be lovable. If I want mercy for me and my children, then I must be merciful to you and yours.

The Dawn of The Age of Enlightenment

For hate and violence only begets hate and violence. The creator says He is not far from us, for in Him we live, move and have our beings (Acts chapter 17:28). It's like a baby being in the mother's womb, drawing all its sustenance from that womb. So we too are in the womb of God drawing our sustenance from God's womb. Our souls have the divine essence of our creator, that essence is love. Love your neighbor as yourselves, and to love our creator with all our hearts, mind, soul, and strength.

The principle is treating each person as we would treat Jesus Christ, if you are a Christian. It is treating each person as Buddha, if you are a Buddhist. If you are a Muslim, treat each as if they were Mohamed the prophet. If you are Jewish, treat each person as if they were our father Abraham It is every religion treating every person with honor and dignity, so that we might walk together, out of the darkness of hate and vengeance; out of the darkness of greed and perversions. Let us build a new world of peace for our children, for they have been left in our care. Let us enable them to fulfill their destinies, let us be better off because we have seen the brightness of their star. Let us not snuff out their lives with the bitterness of war.

Our children were sent into the physical realm to build together, not to blow arms, legs, and heads off their brothers and sisters. The DNA strand cannot lie, from one blood came every nation of men .It is akin to an orange seed, within that seed is the genetic code of all that tree can be. The root system, the trunk of the tree, the bark on the trunk, the branches, the leaves, the stickers, the hurl, the pulp, the skin around the pulp and then in each orange it replicates itself inside the orange fruit 5 to 10 times. How many oranges are produced by that tree that season? Mr. Orange seed is not finished reaching for its maximum potential yet. How many orange seeds will it reproduce the next season and the following seasons? Yet Mr. Orange seed is still not finished reaching for its maximum potential, each seed it has produced ,now can be planted and each seed now have the same potential. Mister Orange seed's potential is unlimited. Are we not a greater creation than an orange seed? If it's potential is unlimited, then why can't we do unlimited things like rebuild the world economy through economic leadership solutions? Economic Leadership Solution is the seed that will show unlimited economic ability in having the world economy reproduce itself in an unlimited way through self-discipline in how we spend our money.

We will delve deeper into this phenomenon in the chapter on the implementation of Economic Leadership Solution. Now we continue to develop the vision of our godhood which teaches us we can do all things through the strength of our faiths. We are more than conquerors through our faith. If we walk righteously, meaning we treat everyone like we want to be treated, then we begin to plant a new seed that will translate us from a world of darkness and all it attributes like war, greed, perversion, disease, and poverty, into a dawn of a new age.

The Dawn of The Age of Enlightenment

I am calling you to a life of self-discipline, a live of service, a life of goodness, of kindness, a life of love. Love simply meaning that I want the best for you and I am willing to do what I can to help you achieve the best for you. There is no mystery in love. Love is deeply caring for each other, and each other's children (no matter where they are found). Let us make our mother Eve proud of us by being unified. By being of a new mind, one that builds the family of nation, not one that blows each other's children up in war, but let each man have freedom of will. Let us break from culture that teaches hate and division, let not our father's wars be our wars. If our fathers refuse to lead toward the brotherhood of man, then let us lead in building a new world order. One where Christians, Muslims, Jews, Hindus, Atheists, Buddhists and all other human beings see each other as brothers from the same blood. Let us recognize that we are brothers from the same ancient mother and father.

Let us be unified, for the enemy of peace knows that united we stand and divided we surely fall. If you would take one small stick, it is easily broken, but if you take a billion small sticks and unify them they will be impossible to break. Eve have over 6 billion off springs. If you can have a new vision with me through ELS we can be an unbreakable global economic system, bound together through unification of brotherhood. Each culture linked together through blood and love, wanting the best for each other.

Economic Leadership Solution

I started prison ministries in two different churches. I worked in soup kitchens, feeding the hungry. I took my sons with my wife and I, letting them see people eating out of garbage cans to survive, and the difference each of my children made when they volunteered to bring out bags of lunches, or served at the soup kitchens. I bring this up to teach a lesson in unification by creating a new mind for our children, that they see themselves as part of the human chain.

I taught for 13 years in detention centers, where the recidivism rate was 80%. That means that 8 out of every 10 inmates release into society would return back to jail. In 13 years I saw only four return back to jail after attending my classes. We taught over 2 thousand inmates during that period. These inmates were from Baltimore, DC and surrounding areas.

What was significant in this phenomenon was that we were creating in them a new mind. We believed that they would plant a new seed, a seed of constructive behavior. We taught them they were not thieves, robbers, drug dealers, or violent men; but that they were eternal being that determined their destiny by how they thought of themselves. For as a man thinks in his heart so is the world he or she creates around themselves like little gods, we are the masters of our fate. If we think of ourselves as a thief when the opportunity comes we will steal, if I think of myself as a man of honor, then I will act as a man of honor no matter what situation I find myself in. If I want to be respected, then I must plant the seed of respect by being respectful to others.

I taught them that if they would walk with me unto knowledge, which brings understanding, when understanding is applied to our everyday life, we become wise, and full of wisdom. I would turn out the lights and it would become dark, and I would say this is life without true knowledge, and without understanding. Without wisdom we stumble around in the darkness. If you stay in the dark long enough your eyes become somewhat accustomed to the dark, and if you and your children stay there long enough you begin to believe that this is your natural state of existence. By the third generation our children won't even believe in the light, and then they begin to accept false truths. They begin to think that the street knowledge is our only way to survive in the darkness. How many men are on death row with the street knowledge? How many men are locked away in these cages call jails for life that are filled with street knowledge? How many families have suffered because of senseless violence? How many are incarcerated because of the gangs which are driven and fueled by the drug trade?

It is time to teach them that we live the lives we create by how we think. We can break this stranglehold of destruction in our communities, in our lives by learning true knowledge, by reaping what we sow, by being constructive and not destructive in our communities. To think from a God point of view, as a spirit being in the physical realm, brings forth the power of God upon this physical realm.

By walking right, talking right, thinking right, we create a new future from a new mind, a mind of responsibility, a mind absent of malice, absent of anything that will caused them failure or excuses to fail. We can do all things through faith which strengthens us.

As I spoke to these prisoners, so I now speak to the family of nations. I urged a new mind of unbreakable unification, spirit beings bringing this God like force to bear upon this physical plane, to usher in a new age ,through how we think. I was being educated by this public broadcasting show, about this theory where the physical world which we learned about in science class was made through the manifestation of atoms, forming the visible world. Atoms are fields of energy manifesting themselves into all forms and phenomenon we experience in the physical realm, we and cars are made from the same stuff Atoms. When these fields of energy are broken down to their original state, we can see them through Atomic microscopes, in this field of energy according to this theory, the energy field that makes up our physical world, changes according to our state of mind, so as it manifest into the world we see and experience, it is influenced by our state of mind.

This was written thousands of years ago in Proverbs 23:7 "As a man thinks in his heart so is he." So we who began to see ourselves as brothers and sisters from the same blood, we began from the very core of our existence to create a new world order of brotherhood. We will not accept the false doctrine of nationhood, which separates us. We will not accept the false doctrine of tribalism which separates us and causes us to be prejudiced against each other. We will not accept any religion that teaches us not to love one another. We will, from the depth of our minds, begin creating, just, and equal societies, where right is might, not how much money you have.

I am calling for kingship of every man, for Queenship of every woman, for Princeship of every boy, and for Princesship of every girl. It is a call to honor, a call to righteousness. It means never treating any female any different than you want your sister or mother treated. Remember they too are eternal being who will transcend from this physical world back to the eternal world from which we all came from. Her creator is your creator. Let us never again dishonor in thought or deed our eternal sisters. We will walk according to the will of God, that is a walk of love,a walk of service, a walk of goodness, a walk of kindness, a walk of power, a walk of justice, a walk of reconciliation, a walk of forgiveness, a walk of peace, a walk of selflessness, a walk of unification, a walk of self-discipline, a walk of truth, a walk of taking wrongs and making them right, a walk of humility, a walk of meekness, which means strength under restraint. It is a walk of worshiping our creator.

It means never being ashamed of our different faiths or never letting our faith injure another faith, or anyone who lacks faith for they too are our brothers and sisters. We will study war no more. We will reject this doctrine of fear which begets mistrust which causes division and leads to war. We will walk as one family solving our problems through economics and respect, you wanting the best for my children, so you plant the seed to get the best for your own children. Eventually those elements of our societies who seek to divide will become the minority, when we the children refuse to blow up our brothers and sisters of other nations, but instead build with them through ELS. We will find that the Bush's and the Bin Laden's will not send their children, nor will they go themselves.

I love my President, and I pray for him, but I will not buy his doctrine of war. He was sent from God to unify the family of nations. War only brings hatred, and hatred is incompatible with God. In this day and time, for God is love, only love can overcome hate. We can build these societies, if we see them as our equals, and love them like we love our own children, and want the best for them as we want the best for our own children. Let not our hearts no longer be hardened, where as in World War II we lost millions of lives because the Germans did not walk in love of their neighbors. War after war we refuse to see the destruction this brings on our children.

The Dawn of The Age of Enlightenment

In America we had slavery for over 300 years and another hundred years of unrepentant discrimination, which gave rise to segregation from the highest legal office in the land; the Supreme Court. The false doctrine of superiority still carries legacies that have helped created our ghettos and have filled our jails. We will speak further on this matter, in the chapter on reparations. Not reparations in the payment terms many are reaching for, I do want to get in their way, but I believe that reparations I speak of will not bring division but unification.

CHAPTER 3

Reparation

S lavery in America has two dimensions. One from the human experience, and the other from the spiritual perspective. I speak as an African American first, then I will speak as the weeping watchmen because sometimes I can't separate the two.

I strive to be the weeping watchman whom God sent to tell the world, that He would love for all men to come unto the knowledge of Him and be saved, and then that human experience of being part of the segregated South until 1965, and going back to see the landmark Supreme court decision legally ending segregation,(Brown vs Board of Education)still had not been implemented in many areas of North and South.

The vestiges of slavery were still standing when I was a boy. Dirt roads, income gaps, education gaps, and opportunity gaps were part of the landscape. Race relations were horrible, the Klan maintained a visible presence. Lynchings and church bombings were commonplace, and were even supported at the highest levels of government. We had Dixiecrats that stifled the progress of black people, in spite of the fact that there were more blacks in governorships and the Senate during reconstruction than we have now.

My great grandfather's grandparents were in slavery. Nearly every black person in my generation knew a grandparent or great grandparent who knew a parent or grandparent who was is bondage .What I must get my nation to understand is that this is a stain upon the soul of our nation before God. It is not just our white brother's problem. It is our problem too.

Oh my African brothers, again our African forefathers were in collaboration with this dastardly deed. Their hands are not clean from this horror. Lives were stolen. Generations after generation, for over 300 years, lives were stolen. Stories are told of our forefathers eating out pig troughs because we were thought of as less than human. People were burned alive in jail cells in the name of vigilante justice. They were lynched, and castrated, and whipped simply because they wanted to be free. Always remember Tulsa, remember Rosewood, Florida, remember the degradation suffered on a daily basis; the dehumanization, and the demoralization of our slave ancestors.

These crimes against humanity have created a wound so infested with hate and division that it will never heal until reparations are paid. The bill is for 300 years of forced unpaid labor, and punitive damages because the after effects are still being endured until today.

These cries from the souls of our enslaved fore-parents for justice have been raised to God the Father, and it has grieved his Holy Spirit. God is a God of patience, and He has given our nation 400 years to repent. Our moment is now! Our moment is now! Our moment is now! Our moment is now! Our moment is now! Our moment is now! Our moment is now! I say it seven times for it is the number of completion, the number of perfection.

What moment you may ask? The moment when we choose life or spiritual death for our nation, whether we choose blessing or curses for our nation. We have no more time to waste. If we continue to allow African ghettos to exist, and jails to overflow with young African American male descendants of African slaves, if we continue to allow the drug trade to flourish sending thousands of these young hopeless men to their graves and on to hell, then we and our children will reap what we have sown in African ghettos and jails.

If we turn a blind eye and act as though we don't see this economic injustice, this judicial injustice, this educational injustice; if we turn a deaf ear to the cries of the African ghettos and act as though we do not hear, we as a nation will suffer the repercussion. It will not just be whites, but our nation as a whole. We thrive together as wise men and women or we perish together as fools. God has seen and God has heard their cries and He continues to hear the cries of the saints that have passed from this physical world into the spirit world.

The ax is at our roots, oh America the beautiful. We can begin to see the unraveling of our appointed place as the leader of nations through our economy collapsing, home foreclosures, crisis in government, multiple wars, and turbulent race relations. Now we are scorned and hated by the majority of the world. We are the largest drug addicted nation, and we produce more pornography and violent entertainment than all other nations combined. Our Children are drawing and using guns in colleges and schools, many of our kids are lazy, selfish, and disobedient. Belligerence is the attitude of the day along with disrespect of elders, and our churches are shrinking numerically.

Our moment is now!!!! What will we choose? Will we continue business as usual or will we right this grievous wrong. Together through economic leadership solution we can build a reparations fund where descendants of slaves will received a $100,000, $50,000 a year, with the monies being spent economically literate. We will set budget directors over these funds. Houses in middle class America will be purchased through ELS. We will create banks, and purchase cars through ELS companies. Every item needed to survive will be purchased through

Economic Leadership Solution

ELS. We will eliminate all the residues of the legacy of slavery, and we will bring into reality our constitution where all men are created by their creator with inalienable rights in the pursuit of the American dream without injustice to people of African descent or any other culture. We will right the wrong (allowing slavery) of our founding fathers.

They will not be the founding fathers of just the whites, but the founding fathers of all nationalities that become legal American citizens. Until this becomes a reality, we will continue to repeat these horror stories that are in every home. The fear of stepping out of place was evident until the 1960's, when the evolution of self-hatred turned into the revolution of black pride. It is time to regain our pride.

What was pressed into the black psyche of 300 years of being considered 3/5 of a human being, 300 years of whippings simply because we wanted to be free, 300 years of selling our children, piercing the soul of a man or woman, slave owners coming into our black women and having their way raping, impregnating and denigrating and devastating their hearts, and piercing the soul of the black woman and the black man because he could not protect her, making him feel even less than a man. Working sun up to sun down for no pay. Making it against the law to educate us, putting us centuries behind on the learning curve must no longer be accepted. We at ELS will not continue just blaming the white man for our terrible dilemma ,for it was the African man that sold us into brutal slavery, and there is some who say the Arab nation, and the Jewish people was part of this unholy alliance. Speaking as the weeping watchmen, I too am a wretched man, seeking forgiveness of my sins.

How can I in good conscience want God to forgive me and then want Him to punish my nation for her sins? God sent me to my nation, to tell her there is no record of wrong in love (1Corinthians 13:8). If we repent and pay restitution, this will show evidence of a contrite heart. Your argument may be to say I was not a part of this crime against humanity. My response would be that if we partake in the riches of this nation then we should pay for the blood spilt and the cruelty of our nation. I believe the African American man in our nation should also pay into the reparations fund. The fund that I envision will not be created from a tax, but from ELS implementation, which finds its foundation in how we spend our sacred dollar. We will explore this deeper in the chapter on ELS implementation.

As a black man in America, let me make it very clear that we have been in America for over 400 years. We have fought in every war; we have been instrumental in building our nation. We take offense when some of the newer immigrants from Europe think they love this nation more than we. We fought in the great Indian wars and in the Mexican- American war and we shed our blood. How dare you come here and think you are more American than the African American nation, when we

Economic Leadership Solution

have been kicked to the curb, economically and socially? Concerning equality, you have been accepted as an equal partner at the economic table, because you were not segregated and put into inferior schools.

Even the Asians and Indians were allowed to integrate, even though we died for this nation, in every war, slaved for this nation when cotton was king, gave rise to many industries, like ship building to carry cotton to Europe, insurance companies to insure slave ships. We are part of the heart of this nation, don't question our patriotism because we feel the injustice of having to look our children in the eyes and tell them we are 2nd class citizens in a nation we have bled and died for even before her conception.

This is why there is such distrust of the leadership of our nation. Instead of chastising us for our bitterness, pray for us, reconcile the education gap with us, reconcile the income gap with us, and elevate us up to 1st class citizens. Understand when we grow up in the ghettos, that we see a continuation of the suffering of our enslaved forefathers. We see the chains of oppression move from our feet to our minds, plagues like poverty, aids violence, teen age and out of wedlock pregnancies permeate our communities, feelings of desperation and hopelessness are epidemic in African ghettos.

School dropout rates should be a national emergency in our nation. I don't blame the white nation for our plight; for I know they are just like the African man trying to do the best for their families. However, when you support without dissent injustice, you are in collaboration with the forces of evil. When you can clearly see the economic injustice to the African people in America, somewhere in the depth of your inner being you must question inequality, glass ceilings, exclusion, and disfranchisement.

It is similar to seeing a child being brutalized by an adult. Something within our inner being, which is called goodwill towards other human beings, moves us without a second thought to rescue that child. Even if it will cause us death, our sense of fair play motivates us as human beings to act. If I watch that child being abused and violated, and I stand by and do nothing but turn a blind eye and act as though I do not see her suffering, and turn a blind ear and act as though I do not hear her cries for help, then I stand by as a certified coward.

If I am not part of the solution to injustice then I am part of the problem, and surely I will answer to God for my inaction and apathy. I blame our nation's leaders for not giving us representation for our taxes. Through ELS we shall overcome these ailments and curses in our communities. If our leaders don't answer the call they shall receive their due reward when they transcend from the physical world to the spirit world.

I voted for Barrack Obama because he says he will change the status quo, where politics are for sale. Unfortunately in the past it has been how much money you can raise for re-election, and that includes both parties. Barrack don't let us down.

I am sending out an urgent call to all my human family to participate in restitution for all the world poor, bringing each child to their maximum potential. We will solve the mounting issues of our day, including creating an alternate economy that will save the earth from which our physical bodies have come from. We will find an alternate to every product that pollutes the earth. It is our charge to take care of her as she takes care of us a symbiotic relationship. For she is alive, how can you plant a seed into something that is dead and expect life to come from something that is dead. Our pollution is making her sick and in return we are becoming more and more sickly. All things are tied together.

Reparations to heal our nation, where wrongs have been committed, we address it head on, not being force to through taxation but through discipline in how we spent our sacred dollars. Not polluting the earth will be our mantra in this new alternative economy, for this new mind that is creating a new world order will be a sound mind, a disciplined mind. I named my first son Nizam, in the Arabic language that means discipline. I knew at 23 years of age that discipline was required to be successful at any endeavor, so as we speak of our three dimensional selves, body, mind and soul, we must understand that there is an internal battle for our destiny. That battle is for the control of the mind, and the battle is between our soul, which is eternal, and our body which is mortal. The one that wins determines the destiny of the man, or the nation.

CHAPTER 4

The Epic War Between The Natural Man And The Spirit Man

The contamination of the mind began for me in my mother's womb. I am hesitant to speak of such issues but the full story must be told, I mean no dishonor to my loving mother or my first hero, my father. However, in order to understand in technical terms the development of our mind, we must flush out all the secrets that lies at the core of psychosis, fears and many human dilemmas.

Psychology is the study of the mind. We must look at this story technically without losing the emotional roller coaster we call the human experience. I will detail out how God uses the frailest of men to do the most extraordinary things. He helped me to believe, even from a young age, that I could rebuild the inner cities.

The Dawn of The Age of Enlightenment

Even today he is helping me believe that I can be instrumental in building the family of nations through Economic Leadership Solution.

I found out years later that my parents were forced into marriage so that my father could travel with my grandmother who was very religious and strict. She was a migrant worker contractor who had worked up north, in New Jersey. My parents were dating, and my father was also dating other women. There was no bond of love, or no bond of trust; the cornerstone of marriage. The foundation for their marriage was built upon the quicksand of accusations, doubts, and character assassination. It was in this world I was conceived.

They say every emotion the mother feels is translated to her forming baby. If she is full of anxiety, full of fear, or full of stress, it transfers to the developing baby. This is the very beginning of the contamination of the developing mind. I don't present myself to be a psychologist, but a man of reason. You tell me if there were doubts from my father that he was my father because someone indicated infidelity by my mother. Can you imagine the vicious arguments? Can you imagine the anxiety, the stress, and the fights probably   physical in nature that came about? it is no wonder I was always fearful, untrusting at my very core. It was no wonder I wet the bed until I was 11 or 12 years of age. It was no wonder I didn't feel comfortable in my own skin. It was no wonder I would have to fight different addictions, like drugs and sexual addictions. My life was ravaged by doubt and insecurity from the very beginning.

I grew up in the rural South where blacks and white children were taught to hate each other, never interacting with each other except in hate. I remember if we were in their neighborhood, they would chase us out, and if they came into our impoverished 'hood we would throw bottles at them, further contaminating the mind of the segregated south.

Born the middle child out of three children, my skin was the darkest skin complexion of the three. In those days we were ashamed of our dark skin, and we thought the lighter you were the more beautiful you were. The old saying was if you are light you are alright, if you are brown stick around, but if you are black stay back. Even though I was brown skinned, in my own home I was made to feel inferior by my lighter skin brother and sister. It became a whipping offense if they called me black or a monkey. We were so full of self-hatred as a race that we boys believed that the pretty pale skin white women on television were too beautiful to even have to take a crap. It sounds insane now, but we believed this brainwashing of their superior race. We could not imagine someone so beautiful on the toilet taking a dump!

The continuation of the contamination of my mind came from being the sickliest of the three children. I almost died at birth, then almost died from can milk poisoning.

The Dawn of The Age of Enlightenment

The more I cried the more milk they would give me. I was told that they had put me in a room to die because they couldn't diagnose me, but thank God for my uncle Frank who suggested that they take me to a major city hospital, which was in St. Augustine, FL, where they saved my life. Because of this experience I gained an aversion to milk. Needless to say I didn't develop big and strong like other young men. I was skinny and small, weighing in at 103 pounds in the 10th grade and topping out at 5'3". I finally asked my brother Tom, why he was growing big and strong, and he said "Steve, I drink a lot of milk." Over my 10th grade summer I drank milk and ate strawberry ice cream like it was going out of style. I grew to 5'8". That is 5" in one summer! I also put on 30 pounds.

I always was too small to ever excel at sports, so I became the water boy so I could travel with my brother's teams in youth league football and middle school basketball. But after I grew, I started a varsity game of football because coach McEvoy really liked my toughness and courage. The JV world practice against varsity and I would stick my head in there against bigger and superior players.

I remember we had a great player, who eventually got a tryout with the Pittsburgh Steelers. His name was Bob Harris, and he was built like Arnold Schwarzenegger. Harris ran the 100 yard dash in 9.8 seconds. I can hear coach McEvoy yelling at him to stop dancing in the hole and to lower his head and run over somebody the next time he got the ball. I always had great anticipation, and was always in the hole before the running back got there. This time Bob Harris lowered his head and barreled towards me with great determination to run over this 133lb linebacker. Bob had to be 225 at the least, and his body looked like Hershel Walker coming through the hole. I lowered my head and collided, I saw stars, and my helmet turned sideways and as I struggled to my feet I saw him lying on the ground unable to get up. As I got to my feet the entire defense and the players sitting on the side line rushed up to me to congratulating me on the hit. At that moment I knew I belonged.

By my senior year I grew 5'11 and ¾ "tall. I left my mark on that team; we went 9 victories and no losses. I became the leader of our defense as left outside linebacker and the signal caller for our defense. My single season tackling record of 16 tackles average per game still stands at Hamilton High in West Township NJ. Later that year as a junior, I made the basketball JV team for the first time and led the team in almost every category.

When one of the guys got kicked off the varsity team, and many of the second years JV players suited up for varsity, I asked Coach Ross to allow me to move up. At first he wasn't excited about bringing another player on the team, but he relented. JV players never played any meaningful minutes, we were just glad to put that Varsity uniform on. After the regular season we qualified for the playoffs, playing Neptune High School in North Jersey in their backyard. We were from Central Jersey; we fell behind by 15 or 16 points in the first half. Little did I know coach Bell, our JV coach, was talking our varsity Coach Ross into putting me into the game. As a kid who was a water boy the year before, it was a when coach Ross called my name to enter the game.

We were going to press them and I would be in the critical part of the press. I was familiar with the press because we ran the same plays on JV, so me and another player named Dickie Rodgers who also had never played turned the game around. I can almost still see me pulling our best player Brian Cain's shirt, pulling him into the correct position in the press. I took leadership in my first meaningful varsity action. We came back and won the game and to hear coach Ross speak to the newspaper about my perseverance, a ball boy from 7th grade to 11th grade.

At that moment my life changed. I earned my starting position for my senior year that game. "Never give up" became my motto for life'. I became a leader that day with my peers had carried that mentality for the rest of my life. Even as I write this book seeking to become a king (a master servant) of the community of nations; even though there are more famous names ahead of me, the ghettos remain, and the curse of poverty remains generation upon generation.

I believe our last king was Dr Martin Luther King. He was my second hero, and he walked us out of segregation. I believe I can walk us out of the poverty of mind, body and soul. Dr King was man of love, who gave his life that we might enjoy the lives many of us live. I believe Economic Leadership Solution will complete the job he was not able to complete because of our contaminated minds.

I really was strong for my size, because I would work on the farm with migrant workers, where on the weekends they would get drunk and we would witness all kinds of violence, homosexuality, and wife beating. I can almost still hear Mrs. Barbara Jean screaming out for help because her husband was beating her out of jealous rages, and no one was interfering. Then we kids began to pick up habits like gambling, pitching pennies, then odd man wins with dimes and nickels, then when we were broke, we began going in the pockets of those migrant workers(men who later became like family because we grew up from childhood to manhood as they grew older) too drunk to notice. We called that clipping, a continuation of exploitation that began with our parents and other migrant work contractors, where when the season of work ran out they build up tremendous debt, so when the work seasons started they owed the contractors nearly all their money which relegated them to slaves. This was further contamination of a mind and developed what I called Karma.

If you exploit the addiction of others for gain, you will set your own children up to be exploited through addiction others will continue this curse through the drug trade setting their children on the road to destruction and exploitation. The curse continues, like those who are victims of child abusers; grow into adults who abuse their children. As we hand down physical ailments in our genetic codes we also hand down spiritual curses, through contamination of the minds that have been given to us by our creator to nurture them to their maximum potential, teaching them to live to the height of the human experience.

We contaminated our own children by our own contamination and we repeat this vicious cycle. Who will rescue us from this vicious cycle? Only through our faith and self-discipline can we overcome. It is never too late! Many times we blame our children's generation for their lack of respect, their foul language, their contempt for authority, and their perversion, but these perversions are a direct result of our own actions as adults. Let us not forget it started in our generation that started in the 1960 with the sexual and drug revolution, and is continuing on until today.

I remember when I was either a 10th or 11th grader we had this party and this minister's daughter had broken up with her boyfriend who was a star on our basketball team. She allowed herself to become so drunk she could hardly walk. I remember these older students took her to one of their houses and raped her over and over as she called out for her boyfriend. Me and some of my friends asked the upper class men to allow us to participate. Sick and contaminated, our unloving minds were at work for the dark side. I thank God today they didn't let us in. She lost her mind that night and was never the same after that. She was a friend that I had known from 5th grade on, and I am ashamed, I pray for forgiveness from her and my eternal father, for not helping, but instead wanting to take part in her mental destruction. But what goes around comes around.

The leader of that rape gang took some PCP, a dangerous drug, and he lost his mind and never been the same ,what goes around comes around. I remember one of the underclassmen on our basketball team, who was probably the nicest guy on the team. He would bring sandwiches for the whole team on away games. One night he took some drug called acid, and tripped out and killed his mother. Again, contaminated minds from a culture of drugs are terrorizing our youth. Our middle linebacker, the best player on our team, a scholarship athlete, put a shot gun in his mouth while suffering from the devastating affect from drugs, and blew his brains out. Another member of our basketball team got lost in drug addiction, overdosed in his parents' home in his bedroom. A victim of no parental authority.

They allowed him to use and would not bother him. They had not seen him come out of the room in several days, then they began to smell an overwhelming stench coming from his room. He had died and now was decomposing. He was rotting to put it more bluntly. Our outside linebacker robbed a store and went on the run to Virginia and hooked up with a friend from the area who was part of one of the largest drug dealers on the East Coast. Because he was so young, maybe 19, he kept getting robbed by this junkie, so he told the leadership about it, and they caught up with the junkie and each one shot him in the head, so no one could tell on any one, and then threw the gun in the Chesapeake Bay. This junkie was in reality an undercover DEA agent.

He ran for a while but eventually surrendered to the FBI. I visited him in jail, and to see him behind bars made me cry. I later learned they turned him into a homosexual. I saw him years later from a distance, and he was too ashamed to come and speak to me. These are not ghetto cases; the African-American ghettos are far more tragic.

This all happened in home owning middle class neighborhoods, I can go on relating tragedy upon tragedy which is the result of contaminated minds, hearts and souls. The lack of male figures in the homes is 90% of the cause of these tragedies many of the children in today's families, especially in the inner cities had to choose between food and shelter, or a male figure in the homes.

During the turbulent 60's riots and unrest caused many businesses to be burned down. That event continues to cause a lack of commerce in the inner cities. The welfare state caused separation of the fathers from their children. We began to slide into the underworld of drug dealing, robbing and going to jail in massive numbers.

Economic Leadership Solution

Mohandas Karamchand Gandhi said if you want to see the oppressed of any nation go to jails, and the oppressed will overflow the penal systems. So when the leadership of our nation could have used the welfare monies to build commerce, like they did for returning vets of WWII ,creating VA loans for education, home loans, building airplane factories and the like. Instead of creating a fatherless welfare state, we could have built a prosperous inner city where men could have had their dignity and honor through their professions, instead of being thieves, and robbers, and drug dealers and the like. That is why I don't blame these boys for their behavior.

I will give you an example from the Animal Kingdom. In one of the nations, Kenya, they built a reserve to save the elephants, because poachers were pushing them into extinction to sell their tusks for the ivory. They put young teenage elephants in the reserve, under the thought process that the younger the elephant the better the sustaining process would be. When they put the young elephants in the reserve, they began chasing giraffes, wilder beasts and all the other animals, making them untenable in the reserve. So they went back to the jungle and got patriarchs, which were older female elephants, who are the leaders of the group (they usually have one bull elephant to seed the group). When they arrived the young elephants fell in line, as they learn how to become elephants. So too will our sons of the inner cities will fall in line, when the patriarchs return home and teach these boys how to be men.

The Dawn of The Age of Enlightenment

These patriarchs I call kings; master servants to their communities who bring love, and respect for authority. Instead of giving them a fish, they are teaching them to fish. These kings must walk according to the will of God. In the Christian faith, we are told that no man can stand against us, if we walk with Him. Our faith tells us we can do all things through Christ who strengthen us. We shall reach into the spirit world for our strength, if we walk according to his will of love, forgiveness and kindness, being our brother's keepers, then all things will work out for the betterment of those who love our Creator, Abba Father in whom we live, move and have our being.

We must root ourselves into righteousness and holiness, which means to be set apart from greed, perversion, laziness, and unbelief. We must tap into this unlimited reservoir of power and potential. Then we will be liken to the caterpillar who crawls on the ground vulnerable to every predator, ugly in appearance before it begins its transformation into a beautiful butterfly, but before the transformation it must break itself out of the dark cocoon, each struggle to break free, it's wings grow stronger and stronger, enabling it to reach its maximum potential, which is to fly above the forest and all its predators. We humans evolve from the aquatic world of our mother's womb.

When the 9 months of formation is complete, the water breaks and you are pushed into the air breathing world. This is our cocoon, here we go through trials and tribulations prey to all predators, but each trial we overcome we are building strong angelic wings to fly above the earth when we are pushed from the air breathing world into the spirit world. We complete a metamorphosis into immortal, incorruptible creatures that live forever. In our trials, will we fall to the predator whose name is fear? Will we be eternally destroyed by the predator named hate, which begot his son named violence, which gives way to a cousin named murder? Or will we rise above these predators and become a beautiful human being that loves and care for his brother, whom can be found in every nation. Overcome with me my eternal brothers and sisters, like the beautiful butterfly who was once an ugly caterpillar, who can't return back to that cocoon, for surely it will die. Let us reach for the height of the human experience, overcoming our once ugliness of division, agreed and perversion and become angelic like creatures.

For as surely as you were pushed from the aquatic world of your mother's womb, you will be pushed from the air breathing world, into the spirit world. Every man, woman or child is appointed to lay down this physical body one day.

If I know I am going on a journey, I prepare for that journey if I am wise. If I was going to drive my car from Florida to California, I would check the car out to make sure it was ready for the trip. I would pack clothes and bring all the items I needed on the journey. I know my soul does not die, but transcends from one dimension that is physical to another dimension that is spirit. The wise man knows that the only baggage he can take with him , are the deeds he has done good or evil. Come and be wise with me and let us build treasures in Heaven by being our brother's keeper. For God said Satan was the father of lies, so He gives us these promises if we love Him with all our hearts mind and souls, with all our strength, with all our might and love our neighbor as our selves.

We must stop the false doctrine of nationality which brings separation, for Christ was not American. He was not Latino, and He was not European. He was every man, every nation, and every tribe. John 3:16 tells us ,for God so love the world that he gave His only begotten son, not just for America, or any singular nation, but for the world to be saved through Him.

We must adapt to this doctrine, not a doctrine of nationality and division. The price for division is too high. We must walk according to the will of God, that is unification, for united we stand and divided we surely will fall. The enemy in the spirit realm who causes division even down to our immediate families knows that if we walk in love, we can bring prosperity to our children. Wouldn't it be so wonderful if we of every nation, every religion and every tribe, can leave behind under our spiritual watch, an everlasting land of peace and prosperity for our children? Through economic leadership solution, we can bring this vision into reality through how we spend money.

Economic Leadership Solution

If we believe we can achieve it, we can, for as a man thinks in his heart so will he be. Will I stand up from my needs of addiction, perversion and darkness of violence whether it be individual, gangs or nations and be the kings and queens, taking our rightful place in the Kingdom of God? We can accomplish this by expressing our unlimited potential as gods (John 10:34- Jesus answered them, is it not written in your law, I said you are gods, that is written in Psalms 82:6). Beings that are eternal in our nature, spirit beings that do not die, but transcend from one world to another, from one dimension to another, from the physical realm of matter and anti-matter to the eternal world of the spirit.

For God is Spirit, and we must bring this power to bear upon our physical world. Then truly we become more than conquerors in brotherhood. So I ask my Jewish brother, my Muslim brother, my Hindu brother, my Buddhist brother, my Taoist brother, and every religious and non-religious brother to come and build with me. Build with me so our children will be proud of us. For we walked out of the darkness of race, creed and all other divisions that hardens our hearts against each other. We stopped selling our sisters, mothers and daughters for profits through pornography, and through prostitution.

Let us treat every woman like we want our mothers and our sisters, and daughters treated. Let us treat them with honor and respect; with dignity, for we are indebted to her, for through woman, God has brought us into this physical world. We owed a debt to her that we can never repay. So I speak to the heart of my brothers, God is not pleased with the way we have treated this precious gift he has given us, through our contaminated minds, she has lost her preciousness to us. Just think for one second what we would be like if God took woman from us.

Now I speak to my sisters, my mothers and my daughters forgive us for our ungracious sins against you, who are the daughters of Eve, the generator of life on this planet. But I am compelled to say to you, you must walk according to the will of God. In the book of Jeremiah, God tells him I knew you before you were created in your mother's womb, which through reasoning tells me that upon conception he was ordained to be housed in that body, if his mother had sacrificed him at the altar of choice, there would have never been Jeremiah the weeping prophet.

I must say this to you because I love you. We as a nation have aborted more than 40 million babies since Roe vs Wade. Many more have been aborted in other nations. If this is the will of Satan, then this spilling of blood, which is the very foundation of life, cries out to God for justice.

I understand all the arguments for prochoice, they are compelling. I have firsthand knowledge in my family the tragedy of loss of life through illegal abortion. My family member bled to death. I know there are thousands of stories like hers around the world. I know there are stories of rape and incest, for the gravity of this dilemma is not loss on me As a young man, I also participated in the decision to end life. My hand is bloody also, and some may say that I don't have the moral authority. However I will give you the example of a recovering alcoholic, he does not have the moral authority to say to someone who struggles with this same addiction to stop drinking, but the whole mission of the alcoholic anonymous organization is to have recovering alcoholics to have sponsors who have been clean for years because they understand the pain of relapse. I know the pain of this difficult decision, so I must ask you, do you think it would have been right for you to have been denied life by your mother and father? No woman except Jesus' mother Mary conceived without a man. I say to all my sisters, no matter what nation we are born in we must find a better solution to this dilemma than spilling innocent blood at the altar of choice.

Together in the spirit of love we can do all things, not me telling you what to do but as I suggest to my brothers to treat you as a special gift from God, to treat you as a priceless gift, I suggest to you to work with me to find better solutions to this dilemma. Like slavery was a curse upon our nation, secretary Rice called it America's birth defect, surely this curse upon the soul of our beloved nation, causing economic disparity even today, creating massive African ghettos in America the beautiful, our sweet land of liberty.

The Dawn of The Age of Enlightenment

This curse causes every nation that loves justice to ridicule our hypocrisy when they see African Americans treated as second class citizens. We lose our moral authority to lead the world. If we lead the world in aborting our children, we curse our nation. Suppose we abort the doctor who was to cure cancer or other major diseases? Suppose we abort the next Mohanda Ghandi, or the next Dr King? Or suppose we abort the next John Kennedy, the next Nelson Mandela, or the next Albert Einstein? What if President Obama's mother had aborted him, and we would not have the first black president.

The dark spirit beings win this dilemma, and we as the family of nations lose. I say to you who are in this dilemma, what would you have wanted your mother and father to do with you while you were in her womb? If you would not mind not having an opportunity at life, then you do what you feel you must, but if you wanted your mother to let you live, then let your baby live. So many people want children and can't have them. Give our next potential world leader a shot at life no matter how difficult that life maybe.

I would want the opportunity to love and lose it than never have experienced love at all. Most people would have loved to experienced life rather than to not have experienced it at all. When we experience life, we fight to survive from death with all our might. We see people overcome miracles dilemmas to live. Even a roach runs when you turn the light on, because it wants to live.

Economic Leadership Solution

Every living entity wants to survive, and thrive, even in the plant kingdom the root system searches the earth for water and nutrients striving to survive. When we play music for our plants they respond to our affection by producing more beautiful flowers. If a plant feels, then how much more can a fetus feel? Nourish it, don't destroy it and toss it in the garbage as though it is a common thing. It is life, striving to express it maximum potential, that of a god, an eternal being seeking its way into the physical realm, to help the human race with its unique mission.

As we all have unique finger prints, we bring unique talents with us from the spirit realm. If we are allowed to see the brightness of their star, we as the human race will be better off if we treat this life form as we want to be treated. You are my sister no matter what decision you make, I will love you and pray for you because we come from the same blood line.

Your mother and my mother are the daughters of Eve, your father and my father are the sons of Adam. We are family, the DNA strand cannot lie. I believe in the Bible and Acts 17:26, from one man came every nation of men. We must grow to love one another even when we disagree with one another. This is the true rhythm of life; it is a vibration, a rhythm syncopation, and soul medication which consists of love, goodness, kindness, respectfulness, integrity, righteousness, purity, servant hood, honorableness, forgiveness, courageousness, truthfulness and Godliness. These attributes are the ticket that allows us to enter into the eternal world. This rhythm of life leads to eternal joy and inner peace deep within our inner being.

The human struggle, in essence, is the battle between self-will and God's will. These attributes are the nature of our souls. Our souls cry out to our minds to be self-disciplined, to walk away from selfishness, but our physical flesh cries out to the mind to live a selfish life that leads to the destruction of the soul. It cries out to the mind to live, drink and be merry, for tomorrow we die. It seeks its own pleasure, self-gratification is it's holy grail, causing such darkness from murder to rape and all kinds of evil and perversion. But the soul cries out to the mind to walk according to the rhythm of eternal life. A life where joy and peace surpasses all human understanding, a life lived at the height of the human experience.

The height of the human experience is joy, peace, goodness, kindness, forgiveness and service; moving on to godliness, which prepares us for that journey that each human being will take one day. For every man is appointed to die one day, to lay this mortal life down. One day our souls will begin that journey. The only things that we can take with us are the deeds we have done. Was I selfless? Or selfish? Did I love my brother? Or was I my brother's keeper. Was I a condemner? Or a forgiver? When my brother was hungry, did I feed him? When he was thirsty, did I give him a drink? When he was sick, did I take care of him? Was I driven by greed

and turned a blind eye to economic and judicial
injustice? Did I turn a deaf ear to the cries coming from
Africans in American ghettos and jails? Their fore
parents suffered 300 years of slavery, and another 100
years of unrepentant discrimination.

God is a God of patience; He has allowed 400 years to
repent. I cry out to the minds of our nation from my
soul. Let us allow our souls to determine our destiny, not
our flesh. For which ever, the flesh or the soul controls
our minds, controls our destiny. I say to the church, to
the synagogues, the mosques, the Buddhist temple, we
must be watchmen over the souls of our nations. We
must debate in love the merits of our faiths, and agree to
disagree in love, yet out of that love we must follow the
creeds of our faiths. That is to spread the good news of
our faiths and to let each individual have the inalienable
right to choose their own eternal destinies. Each faith
must be confident that their faith will be sustained
through spiritual debate, as they did in the cities of light
of Spain, under Muslim rule at the turn of the first
millennium. We thrive together as brothers and sisters
no matter what our faiths.

If we don't, we perish in our own self-interest. God sent
me to you to tell you there is no record of wrong love,
for love is patient, love is kind, love seeks out and loves
the truth, love never fails. God is love. God sent me to
say it is now time for us to build together the family of
nations, not me leading you or you leading me, but side
by side we will build a new world order for each other's

children, preparing for that appointed day when we lay this mortal life down and be raised up immortal, neither male nor female, but the spirit beings going to meet the deeds we have done good or bad.

I must speak to you about homosexuality reluctantly, because I can hear my readers already calling me a bigot. First of all gay men and women are my sisters and brothers. We come from the same mother and father, I love you no less than I love my straight brother sister, whom I believe to be in sin, for I too am a sinner so I set in judgment of no man, but God's word set in judgment of every man. Homosexuality is found in no creature that God created except man. I believe this dilemma to be one of the most difficult crosses to bear in the human experience. Every child who struggle with their sexuality, is tormented by the demonic spirits until it breaks them, knowing they could lose family and friends. I don't believe this is by choice, I believe this is a powerful delusion sent by the prince of the dark world. I believe many victims are attack by this dark force in their infancy. Like the woman says the men in these FLDS cults break babies before they can establish long term memory, for if you can confuse the child before his sexual identity is established, then he or she believes these thoughts emanate from within themselves. The master deceiver who has no mercy ,no sense of fair play, knows if he corrupts our minds early he will have us in the strong delusion until the truth set us free. I say to my gay brothers and sisters, if this was a natural phenomenon and everyone turns gay before all the intro fertilization came about, mankind would have ceased to exist. My heart goes out to those who have to deal with this strong delusion.

I believe that no man should look down on our gay sisters and brother. I believe this emotion or attraction to the same sex is normal, as long as it is not lust. In the emotional realm, to have a friend that emotions run as deep as any emotion for the opposite sex like King David and Jonathan in the bible, their love was as deep as any humans could have for another, but the enemy of mankind perverts something that is pure and genuine.

I remember I had a friend named Jerry. We hung together almost every day from 7th grade until I met my wife at age 22. We went to electronic school together, went to California after graduation at age 19 together, and chased women together. He was part of my heart, we never argued, and we got along better than me and my wife ever got along. I remember we went from California to New Jersey to Tampa, looking for technician jobs. That is where I met my wife, we all disc jocked together. We let her into our inner circle. I remember Jerry being jealous of my affection for her and tried to hit on her behind my back to test her. They didn't get along. When I knew Jerry was no longer going to be a part of my life I cried, never no sexual feelings but a deep and affectionate love for each other. That is what we are supposed to have without the dark deception that leads to spiritual death. According to the word of God, I believe Oprah and Gail have such a beautiful relationship like that, we even feel jealous of other relationships with our friends. I just wanted to give another prospective to one of life's greatest dilemmas.

I must say that my gay brothers and sisters are some of the most talented and nicest people that I have ever met. I love your souls so much that that I am willing to be rejected by you and scorned by you and called all kind of names by you or you can disagree with love and respect. You fight one of the greatest battles of mankind I will cheer for you and encourage you; never will I look down on you for we are family, born from the same blood.

The DNA strand cannot lie. You are my sisters and brothers and I speak from my heart of love to the gay nation. Together through economic leadership solution we will build the family of nations, side by side, not me leading you or you leading me, but side by side in brotherhood, even if you choose to remain sexually active. We still welcome you to build the family of nations together, like a friend who commits what I consider other sin, my love for you will always remain. I will hate the sins in my life, because I too am a sinner seeking forgiveness of Christ, but I know I must walk according to His will and not my will. This is the choice of life. He says I lay before you life or death, blessing or curses, as for me and my household we will choose life.

Let me share my thoughts on the historic race for the presidency in the 2008 election. I as an African

Economic Leadership Solution

American am torn between my cultural roots and my eternal roots. My cultural mind that of an African in America leaps for joy at the threshold of seeing our nation fulfilling the promise of our constitution that all men are created equal with the same rights and privileges to pursuit happiness from a just and equal society, yet I watch with sadness as I see elements in our society that wants to derail this moment in our sacred racial history.

First let me say, I speak to my white brothers and sisters in love. I raised my family in Frederick, Maryland. I attended Frederick Church of Christ, 99% mostly white because I lived in the suburbs of Washington DC. I consider two of my best three friends to be white, we raised our children together. I taught their children in Sunday school and they taught mine. We started soup kitchens, prison ministries, and raised money for the MD together. They have financially and emotionally help me through some dark days in my life, and been there for me more than my own blood relatives. I am now and always will be in love with Frederick Church of Christ, which is 99% white.

I am not deluded by Satan's schemes of division of race and creed, when love is planted in your heart. Only love can germinate from that seed of love. I had to decide whether I was a Christian or a black Christian. I decided to be a Christian. This is my call to every white, black, Hispanic, Asian and Native American Christian, decide like me to be Christian first, and we will eliminate

The Dawn of The Age of Enlightenment

Sunday at 11 o clock, being the most segregated hour in our nation. I sacrificed the wonderful black church experience, from most of my Christian life. When I was able to attend some black churches I loved and was overwhelmed by the spirited singing, the amens, the black theme preaching, never blaming the white nations for all our ills, but placing blame at Satan's feet for our battle against the dark forces of the spiritual realms that enters our heart and deceived us into not loving one another.

I speak to my nation from this background; this election was monumental on many levels. First it declared to the whole world that we have passed from second class citizens to first class citizen. We would never elect a second class citizen to be most powerful man in the world, so there is rejoicing around the world. People will see America living symbolically its creed, we are the hope of the whole world. Global economies depend on our economy.

There is a saying, that when America sneezes, the world catches a cold. What a privilege to be born by the will of God, to be the greatest nation in the history of the world, when much is given, much is required, we must not basked in creed while the world languishes in poverty

Our number one killer is obesity and all the ills that flow from this malady. We over eat while other parts of the world's children dig in the ground for roots to eat. This breaks God's heart, this is why the election was so critical. It gave hope to all mankind, not just America, but our enemies gave pause to have a look at America. We were able to seize that moment in history, so we can bring world peace with America leading the way.

God tells us to pray for our enemies to want the best for them and their children then they would want the best for us and our children. What goes around comes around. I am not living in a fantasy world in these hopes as we change our paradigm of how we see the world, and then the world will change its view of us. If we see each nation as a brother and sister nation, then they will slowly begin to see us in that same brotherhood of nations.

But there is an enemy that never wants us to use the spirit power of unity to change a dying world. Their economic interest would be at stake, but will we the children of Eve continue to be deceived, or will we bring about the dawn of the age of enlightenment and break this strangle hold of self-interest and begin to bring a spirit force grounded and rooted in love one for another no matter what nation we are from. When one of God's children is hungry then we should feel their hunger pain as if our own children are hungry.

If President Obama fulfills his destiny by promoting world peace and world prosperity not one nation under God but all nations under God then we will see peace. We must resist fear and not let it be the foundation from which we think, we must strain with all our might from these old prejudices, like being in the weight room straining to lift 200lbs. We must strain with all our might to press forward and stop looking backward. We can't change the pass, but we can build a new future together, me looking out for your children and your children looking out for mine, never letting the dark forces harden our hearts that we turn a blind eye and deaf ears to the suffering of children, we must not allow ourselves to get into a rat race mentality, a me myself and I mindset.

Secondly he represents hope for every black boy and girl that we can achieve anything in our great nation, if we be self-disciplined, study hard, and stay out of trouble. What a symbol! A kid born to a teenage mother, a father who abandoned them at age 2, on welfare, help raised by his grandparents, most black boys or any poor kid of any race will see that see that they can achieve anything. Older African Americans will feel so much pride in America. Most African Americans felt what Michelle Obama expressed when she spoke of being proud of her country for the first time.

If you have been treated like a second class citizen in your own nation, feeling left out of the American family, only being allowed into the mainstream society by voting rights law and affirmative action laws, you still feel unloved and emotionally left out. You still feel that people don't respect your contribution; you feel that people think you to took some deserving white person's position or scholarship.

Economic Leadership Solution

If you are white you will never understand Michelle, but we as blacks understood her completely. To see whites in Utah, and North Dakota vote for President Obama blew our minds and made us feel loved and wanted. It almost made me cry, for we have loved a nation that have not loved us, our blood have been shed in every war before most immigrants of European ancestry came in the late 1800 and early 1900. To hear them question our patriotism is infuriating and counterproductive.

We see them because of the color of their skin integrate into mainstream society, reaching the highest levels of accomplishments through hard work and sacrifice, when we complain that our hard work and sacrifice have not rendered the same results, who are you to question our patriotism. Whites have never been segregated from the rest of society, as though you were unfit to integrate, as if their children were better than our children. How insulting to a proud people, these wounds run deep and wide.

President Obama is like a healing balm to our wounded psyches. I don't expect the media to understand this. How many black talking heads do we have on television that host main stream cable network news? Little to none. There is an old saying you can't judge a person until you walk a mile in their shoes. This schism of race has a life of its own. It must and will be slain. We have sacrificed too much heartache and pain at the altar of hate and fear, these demigods will and must die, to more perfect our imperfect union.

The Dawn of The Age of Enlightenment

CHAPTER 5

A Call To Our Celebrities

I call to Queen Oprah to come and build with me a new world order. I call you Queen Oprah, not because you are Queen of the airwaves through ratings. I call you Queen because you are a master servant, because of your love, you created a girls school in South Africa that serves and will continue to serve what will facilitate thousands of African girls to reach their maximum potential. That and other projects of service are evidence of your love, born out of your heart for the family of nations. God sends His honor to you, for he says there is no greater love when someone lays down their life for a friend.

When you lay your money down, you are laying a piece of your life down, because it took sacrificing your life to achieve the money you have earned. To explain clearer, when we work 40 hours a week for a paycheck we have sacrificed 40 hours out of our lives we will never get back, so thank you Queen Oprah for your loving sacrifice, but your job is not over yet.

We have a new society to build through Economic Leadership Solution. We will bring our god-like power to bear upon this physical realm, and change the world through building life centers throughout the family of nations. We will buy and sell economically literate, every product and service we use and every customer that uses you Queen Oprah, as his or her reason that they buy economically literate, we will give to your foundation 90% of our profits. That could grow into billions of dollars annually. How many more projects and life centers we can build together? Overnight we can generate through your celebrity, millions of economically literate consumers.

I was sent into this physical world to unite the family of nations through Economic Leadership Solution. I believe if we love our neighbor as we love our own families there is nothing we cannot accomplish, including rebuilding our inner cities by creating commerce and a new mind through this dawn of the age of enlightenment. We will teach them together that they are gods, eternal beings; not drug dealers, robbers, killers, or violent and perverse people, but men and woman made in the image of God. We unlimited in our potential, when we are self-disciplined and focused. Queen Oprah my hope is that you will hear my call and become part of the Economic Leadership Solution family. I await your Call Queen Oprah!!

Economic Leadership Solution

I call King Bill Cosby. Bill I call you King because you and Queen Camille have sacrificed so much money to higher education. You have stood the test of time with your devotion to the African American cause. I have had over the years many dreams of you; it is as if I knew you from another time and place. In my dreams you were my best friend.

My hope and prayers is that you and Queen Camille will come and build with me this new world order by simply using your celebrity status to get Economic Leadership Solution in the door of corporations and colleges. We will create a pin # for your ELS foundation and we will partner with you and donate to all foundations and organization 90% of our profits that come from your leads. ELS will partner with all foundations, organizations and companies. 90% of its profits will go back to the communities that generate these revenue streams.

Imagine King Bill, the new life centers we can build, paying our professors $400.000,$500.000,$600.000 dollars a year, bringing minds from the family of nations and teaching in the inner cities, at the highest levels of science ,art, mathematics, and sports competition, all spiritually minded and Christ centered. Like Dr King, I am not ashamed of my faith. I believe it teaches self-discipline and self-respect as well as respect for others. I believe it is a secret weapon we have lost.

The Dawn of The Age of Enlightenment

The power we gain from the eternal world is missing in many of our lives and the lives of our children. That is why we see the condition we see today. One might argue we have so many church buildings, a church building on every corner, but I must submit to you that like counterfeit money that has no buying power, counterfeit churches have no Godly power. Many of our ministers have committed adultery. Homosexuality is rampant in the ministries, we have ministers chasing little girls and little boys, and we have ministers on drugs, and chasing prostitutes. It is no wonder the pulpit of Christ has been robbed of its power and now because of this behavior men of God are being mocked and ridiculed.

ELS will not throw the baby out with the bath water. God will send true men of God to help build Economic Leadership Solution, because I believe we create our future by how we think and act today. We will reap what we sow. We will sow true honor, true integrity, true courage, and true vision, for without it we perish.

We at ELS are asking all counterfeit ministries, who prostitute the church for their personal gain of fortune and fame, to step down from the pulpit. God will not be mocked! Let Christ minded, not worldly minded, men of God take their rightful places as we usher in this new age of enlightenment.

I call on every Church to become unified in the Kingdom of God. King Bill, God has sent me to call you to this challenge to unite the family of nations. We will build ELS first in the inner cities first, then the rural areas, capturing the money that is due from the forced unpaid labor of our slave ancestors, without taxes and division, simply raising this money by how we spend our money. I believe it is your destiny to come build with me." I await your call King Bill"

I call to Tiger woods, Economic Leadership Solution will bring to reality what your father prophesied about you, and that is that you would change the world. Through your worldwide fame you can bring in close to a billion economically literate consumers and businesses. Your foundation will generate billions. That is money to change the poor Asian nations, making your mother proud. Helping rebuild the ghettos will make your father's spirit so proud and cancel the ridicule he endured by having such a grand vision for you. I know he will be vindicated if you hear the call of ELS, bringing millions to economic literacy, and creating a multi-trillion dollar world economy to do great works in your father's and mother's name. What an honor it would be for you, Tiger, to be in the life hall of fame. I await your call!!

I call to Michael Jordan, who I nicked name the economic Moses of our time, you moved the stock market over 10 billion dollars in your prime. You were given an indomitable will to win, now we need that will to help build the family nation. You were in training and perfecting your indomitable will when you won 6 NBA championships, nearly pushing yourself to the brink of death during the Utah championship series. MJ we need that indomitable will to build a new and just society. We need you to lead up to the championship of life and become the king God created you to be. MJ come and build with me and find your destiny. I await your call!!

Magic Johnson I call you to come build with me, for we need your strength. Magic, you were the first to look HIV in the face and you stared it down. Magic we need your strength to overcome stubborn minds as you continue to overcome this stubborn virus. Magic I call you to a Holy life, obviously you are precious in God's sight, to give you second life, is He precious enough in your sight to help me to build a new world order? A life where children in Africa will not have to dig roots out of the ground to survive, while our children eat when they want and as much as they want. Help me to usher in a new age of enlightenment, when we can love poor children of every nation as we love our own children. Magic, through your celebrity, which was ordained by God when he gave you from birth unique talents and through your hard work you perfected them. But you can't perfect 6'10', that is God given, you can't perfect basketball IQ, that is God given. Magic everything you touch turns to gold, come join ELS and bring that Midas touch. I am awaiting your Call!!

I call Will and Jada Smith to fulfill your destiny, and that is to come and build a new world order with me. As I watched 60 minutes on June 29, 2008, and heard you are seeking to change the world, I knew then you were being called by God to an extraordinary work. For the platform you have been given, was preparing you to be an extraordinary King, a master servant in building a new world order with me. I was inspired by the story you told about your father, issuing an edict for you and your brother to build that wall in front of his refrigeration business. The lesson you learned was that there is nothing you can't do if you put your mind to it.

That lesson must be taught to a dying and desperate world. My father taught me similar lessons of work ethics. I have also seen how celebrity didn't change you with your friends and I have seen the love of what seemed like a former teacher that she still carries for you. I call you to be a leader in the ELS revolution. I call you to be a lead spokesperson for ELS, and to apply the lessons you learned in building a super star entertainment career. You were in training to fulfill your true destiny as an eternal being sent upon this physical realm, to build our inner cities and our rural areas, creating commerce through Economic Leadership Solutions like the celebrities of the 60's. Blacks and whites stood beside Dr King, a prophet of love. So too I ask you, Will and Jada, to stand beside me, to use your celebrity which is God given, to its maximum potential. Do not let celebrity use you as so many of your peers do.

When celebrity is not used for its correct purpose, it brings destruction of mind, body and soul. This is why we see such personal destruction in our celebrities. They believe their rising star is in and of themselves, and they are sadly deceived and the destruction of marriages and their children is evidence of this false belief. Will, when I heard you say you want to change the world, here at ELS you will find your destiny. Here you will fulfill your maximum potential to build a new world order, where love is the motivating force that drives us and not greed. A new world order where compassion and loving kindness and tender mercies toward those less fortunate than us, is the foundation we will build. Will Smith I will be honored to serve the family of nations with you. I excitedly await your call!!

I call my brothers Tom Joyner, Mike Basyden, Steve Harvey, Travis Smiley, Roland Martin and other brothers and sisters in the black broadcasting association. You were placed in these positions, not for vain glory but to help build a new world order. I call to you brothers and sisters because I admire you for your love of our community. Through Economic Leadership Solutions we will rebuild our communities. We will create a new mind of success through education and commerce, which will bring jobs, which births dignity and honor and respect. If you would give me a platform from your shows, we can begin to build a new world order.

Each person I call will be rewarded in the physical world and the Spirit world. Come and find your destiny with me, not me leading you, or you leading me, but side by side, shoulder to shoulder marching with one mind, one purpose to rise our people from second class citizenship to first class citizenship. Never let us ever again have to look at our children in the eyes and tell them we left them as second class citizens in our nation or any nation on this earth.

My brothers and sisters in the broadcast industry, you are the key to building ELS, you are the key, this is our Holy grail. To rescue our sons and daughters from self-destruction and to teach every one of them how to be young men and young women. We can create billions of dollars without asking our government for not a dime, (just the amount of contracts due to us equal to amount we pay in taxes) but by our economic literate spending habits. We can change the game to our advantage. We never again need to go hat in hand begging anyone, at any time to help us out of this devastation we find in our community. We were born to be Kings, to rise above circumstances and to be all we were created to be, with unlimited potential expressing itself through loving our neighbors and our nation and then the family of nations, through vision and hard work I excitedly await your call.

I call to you Queen Alicia Keyes, to come build a new world order with me. For your good works has elevated you to be adorned with the crown of Queenship. Your works in Africa touch the core of my inner being. I will be honored to have you as a spokesperson for Economic Leadership Solution. Queen Alicia, ELS is liken to a magnifying glass in the sunlight, it takes the sunlight and manifest it to its maximum potential.

The Dawn of The Age of Enlightenment

Let me explain, if you take a magnifying glass and put it above your head and position it between your hand and the sun, it will magnify the sun's potential until it burns the back of your hand. The only difference is the magnifying glass has streamlined the sun to reach for its maximum potential. ELS will be like the magnifying glass in fulfilling the economic potential of our community.

$800 billion we spend a year in products and services and we get nothing back significantly from the companies we enrich through our spending habits. Queen Alicia, if we charge a company 10% for every economic literate customer we send them (monies these companies spend on their advertisement budgets anyway) we can generate through discipline spending $80 billion a year for our community. ELS will return 90% of our profits to our communities.

This will enable us to create commerce in our ghettos and the penal system, by building call centers there and let the inmates take a third of their earnings and pay for detention and pay into a victim fund and they get to take care of their families and save the rest. Everyone being drug tested and any acts of violence takes them off the program. This is true rehabilitation. Queen Alicia, I am a true admirer of yours and my prayer is that you will heed this personal call. I await your call!! Urgent!

I call my white brothers and sisters like Brad Pitt, Angela Jolie, Hillary and Bill Clinton, Rush Limbaugh,

Economic Leadership Solution

Sean Hannity, Larry King, Tom Brokaw, Britney
Spears, Paris Hilton, Lindsay Lohan, Keith Obberman,
Steve Colbear, George Cloney, Tom Cruise and all my
white brothers and sisters celebrities whom I have not
named, if you love justice and equality hear my call!!.
Steven Spielberg, you can help us at ELS, by making a
movie about ELS; making a movie about an African
boy, coming up out of the ghetto experience of drug
dealing, and gang banging, standing up from his knees,
from addiction, creating a great wealth for himself, and
returning to the ghetto to show former gang bangers how
to sell cutting edge technologies. Dressing like corporate
America: clean cut, shirt and tie, in a drug free work
place, taking random drug tests to show we are away
from the scourge of drugs and all the darkness that goes
with it.

This younger brother, along with his new found friends
from every culture teaching how to achieve the
American dream. I would love to see a collaboration of
Eddie Murphy, Spike Lee and Ron Singleton each take
part in bringing this vision to the big screen. If we can
see, we can believe it, and if we can believe it, we can
achieve it. I await your call!! Urgent!

I call Jay z and Beyonce. I call our President Barrack
and Michelle Obama, I call Denzel Washington and his
wife, I call Kobe Bryant and his wife. I call Labron
James and all the NBA . I call Dereck Jeter and all major
league baseball. I call Wayne Gresky, Kid Sid and all
the rest of the NHL, to walk with us in building a new

world order where every man and woman is created equal. I call to LT and his wife, I call to Brett Farve and his wife and to the rest of the NFL to come build with us at Economic Leadership Solution. I call on Democrats and Republicans to build with me. In our life time we leave an enlightened world to our children, a world of peace and honor to all nations under God, a true brotherhood of mankind.

CHAPTER 6

The Failure Of The Church

You may as what the Holy Church has to do with economic literacy and why in a book that calls for the brotherhood of all faiths, why do you single out the Christian faith to chastise? And I must say to you that I am of this particular faith and I am compelled to speak to my spiritual family through love, as my brother Apostle Paul spoke to the Corinthians, to the Galatians and to the other churches that became divisive. Because if no other takes up the challenge to build a new world order, my hope is that the Christian Church will heed my call to build a new world order that demands us to love and pray for our enemies and our neighbors. It is the mission statement of the Christian faith. So I must speak to her individually, but the concept is the same for all the world's great religions.

When the Church sits in judgment of God's servants who don't agree with our doctrine as we interpret it, we breed contention and division, acting in a manner that is opposite what Jesus prayed for in the 17th chapter, where He prayed for unity, that the Holy Church would be one as He and the Holy Father is one. I am compelled to ask you to think deeply about this contention and division, where denomination after denomination condemns one another to hell if they don't agree with every letter of the law of their particular doctrine.

Jesus said we are the light of the world, a dark dying world. He said we are the salt of the earth, and we are his ambassadors on earth, so I must ask the leadership of God's Holy Church, "What does the world see when they look at the Holy house?" This light that shines in this dark world, do they see the holy Catholic Church condemning the Holy Baptist Church? Do they see the Holy Baptist Church condemning the Holy Church of the Seventh Day Adventist? Do we see the Seventh Day Adventist condemning the Holy Kingdom of Jehovah Witness? Do we see the Witness condemning the Holy Charismatic Church? and do we see my church, the Holy Church of Christ condemning all Holy Churches that don't agree word for word with our doctrines? Do they even say that others who hope in Christ, worships in vain.

In all faiths that walk in this arrogance, beware for the word of God teaches us that we shall be judged with the same measure that we judge. That is why he who says who are any of us to judge his servants. Only God and that servant knows the intent of that worshiper's heart, that is why He said let the wheat and barley grow together and let God's angel at the end of the world separate them.

In Romans 8:1, God says there is no condemnation in Christ Jesus. If we continue to be divided, how can we teach a divided world unity? If they look at our condemnation of each other, how can they see the love of God in us? How can we teach the world when they look at us and see division and condemnation? They don't see the Holy Church that Jesus, the Lamb of God purchased with His blood, they see the world.

Jesus says his disciples will be known by their love one for another. Condemnation is not love, and ridiculing each other is not love. This mentality is not of humility. Thinking others as better than our selves is true humility. He who puts himself first shall be last in the Kingdom of God, and he who sits himself at the head table will be humiliated when the master of the house comes and asks him to be seated least at the table.

Would it not be more rewarding to sit at the least most important seat at the table, and when the master of the house comes he reward you with the most important seat at the table? I can almost hear the leadership of the Holy Churches saying, I believe in particular doctrine and I will never change it for anyone, and I say Amen. I will never leave the Church of Christ, but I will not condemn no church that believes that Jesus is the son of God that died on the on the cross of Calvary for the sins of the world, reconciling those who believe on His name, back into a right relationship with God, giving us the power to be called the children of God and that he rose from the grave on the third day and now sits on the right hand of God. You are my brother if you profess Ephesians 4:2-6.

Ephesians 4:2-6 King James Version (KJV)

[2] With all lowliness and meekness, with longsuffering, forbearing one another in love; Endeavouring to keep the unity of the Spirit in the bond of peace. There is one body, and one Spirit, even as ye are called in one hope of your calling; One Lord, one faith, one baptism, One God and Father of all, who is above all, and through all, and in you all.

Ephesians 4:2-6 New Living Translation (NLT)

Always be humble and gentle. Be patient with each other, making allowance for each other's faults because of your love. Make every effort to keep yourselves united in the Spirit, binding yourselves together with peace. For there is one body and one Spirit, just as you have been called to one glorious hope for the future. There is one Lord, one faith, one baptism, and one God and Father, who is over all and in all and living through all.

So I know that every Church no matter what denomination or non-denomination believes this. All Christian's believe that Jesus is the son of God. No Christian Church refuses to believe that He suffered and died under Pontius Pilate, and no Christian Church does not believe that He didn't rise from the dead on the third day.

Acts 2:33 says, and that He sits at the right hand of God mediating on our behalf. no Christian Church refuses to believe Acts 2:38-39, that we must repent and be baptized (buried in the watery grave symbolizing when Jesus was buried in the tomb. He rose from the tomb in His heavenly glory, so to we rise from the watery grave of baptism, new creatures, no longer of this world, only in it to help save it).

Every one of you believes in the name of Jesus Christ for the remission of sins and you shall receive the gift of the Holy Ghost. Acts2:38-39 tells us that each one of you must turn from sin, return to God and be baptized in the name of Jesus Christ for the forgiveness of your sins, then you shall receive the gift of the holy Spirit, for Christ promised him to each one of you who has been called by the Lord our God and to your children and even to those in distant lands.

Oh Holy Church it is time for us to unify, for we have a new world order to build. United we stand and divided we fall. If we unite, there are approximately 1 billion Christians who hope in Christ, through economic leadership solutions, we can wipe out hunger. We can get medicine so no child or adult will die from preventable diseases. We will bring clean drinking water to every nation.

We can do all things through Christ who strengthen us. (Ephesians 4:13). Romans 8:31-32 says ,"what can we ever say to such wonder things as these? If God is on our side who can be against us? Since he did not spare even His own son for us, but gave him up for us all, won't He also give us everything else?" Romans 8:37, for in all things we are more than conquerors through him that loves us.

Oh! Holy Church, I need you now to be one!!!! I say to the leadership of every house of God, if your church building was on fire and someone from a different denomination or no-denomination comes with a bucket of water, would you turn him away? I say surely you would not. I must say to you, our communities are on fire with drug addictions, perversion on every corner in many ghetto cities. Gang murders and violence driven and fuel by the drug trade ruin our communities. There is no respect for authority in our schools; our colleges are turning into Sodom and Gomorrah. Teenage pregnancies, out of wedlock children, and children being disrespectful and disobedient to their parents plague our neighborhoods. Violence is rampant, plagues like aids and other sexually transmitted diseases are reaping havoc on our children, God's lost sheep, while we fight among ourselves over non salvation issues.

Economic Leadership Solution

The enemy is destroying our children and our communities. I can almost hear Rama crying through the corridors of time that her children is no more, while we sit in the pews every Sunday condemning each other's doctrines, when all of us believes the gospel of Jesus Christ. I am compelled to ask you, oh Holy Church, who wins in our divisiveness?

Surely not God, so this championing of our own doctrines of division helps the enemy. The enemy knows better than we, for united he falls and divided he wins. So I say to each denomination and non-denomination, don't change your worship service for me, for I will never change my worship service for anyone, but what we can do is unite economically, communicatively, and socially, being of the same mind to seek the lost through building life centers which are spiritually minded and Christ centered schools where we will pay our teachers and professors hundreds of thousands of dollars annually, to bring the brightest minds to teach our children the greatest knowledge in the world.

Each denomination can teach each doctrine at the life centers they help build through their own sacred spending habits. United we shall stand!!!!

The Dawn of The Age of Enlightenment

Psalm 133

A song for pilgrims ascending to Jerusalem. A psalm of David.

^{1} *How wonderful and pleasant it is*
when brothers live together in harmony!
^{2} *For harmony is as precious as the anointing oil*
that was poured over Aaron's head,
that ran down his beard
and onto the border of his robe.
^{3} *Harmony is as refreshing as the dew from Mount Hermon*
that falls on the mountains of Zion.
And there the LORD has pronounced his blessing,
even life everlasting.

In the church there are one billion confessing Christians.
That means a tenth is 100 million to plant that Holy
seed). As Jesus revolutionized the religious leadership of
his generation, we the anointed, are now calling to
prepare the way for his second coming, as John The
Baptist prepared the way for his first appearing.

He shall find his bride whole, held together by the
ligaments of love and forbearance, not teaching the letter
of the law, but the Spirit of the law, for if our teachings
do not motivate each Christian to be obedient to Apostle
Matthew teaching in Matthew 25:31-40, a call to feed
the hungry to clothe the naked, to care for the sick, to

visit those in prison, to bring the good news of the Gospel, then all our teaching is in vain. For when He separate the sheep from the goats, these are prerequisites to enter Heaven's door. So I, the weeping watchman issue this calling to the anointed: come unify with me, forsaking division, letting God be God, (for it is a dangerous to sit in God's seat, judging his servants) separating the righteous from the unrighteous in doctrinal matters and embracing unity through economic leadership solutions. A vehicle of service and reconciliation in Jesus name!

CHAPTER 7

Implementation Of Economic Leadership Solution

Economic Leadership Solution implementation starts with the fundamental belief that the only true power we have is how we spend our money. This idea at its basic concept is a symbiotic relationship between the consumer and the merchant that starts from the precept that we both will benefit from our business relationship in a win-win proposition.

Most major companies spend approximately 10 % of their revenue on their advertisement budgets through marketing which includes TV, radio, newspaper ads, movies, Internet and other marketing outlets, to entice the general public to buy their products and services. The part Economic Leadership Solution plays is to be a conduit contractually with these companies, as a contractor to sell their products and services through our enterprise which is an E-commerce company. We in return, through our communities buying all products and services from ELS, will partner with our communities. 90% of our profits will be returned back to the communities and its organizations to rebuild our own communities and to begin to solve their pressing issues of the day. ELS will return 90% of its profits back to the communities and its participating institutions and organizations to build new schools which ELS will rename as life centers.

Our concept is simply spiritual re direction on how we spend our money. We don't ask any consumer to expand their budget by spending one red cent more than they currently are spending. With business as usual, we get nothing back to significantly change our ghettos and rural poverty stricken areas.

For example if you are going to buy a cell phone and its service, buy it through our company and we ask the service provider for a maximum that will grow to 10% for every customer we send them that buys economically literate, which is the same concept as being computer literate. You gain the maximum potential of each dollar we spend.

In the African American community, we spend over 800 billion dollars a year and get nothing significant back for enriching these corporations. If we spend that money economically literate, we can generate 80 billion dollars a year. Then we can begin to rebuild our infrastructure, build life centers that are spiritually minded and that teach our children self-discipline and values like a strong work ethic, respect for authority and other core values that lay a foundation for success and living out the American dream.

Out of these 80 billion dollars we will bring the most brilliant professors, the brightest minds in the world to teach at these life centers. We will pay them three, four, five hundred thousand dollars a year to get them there, whatever it takes.

Our children will start at 4 months old to begin developing their minds to reach their maximum potential. They say a child develops their learning capacity 80% by age 4. They learn the language, personality traits and a number of other coping mechanisms by age 4. We will develop their spiritual potential, teaching them love and service to their neighbor, teaching them they are eternal beings upon this physical realm, sent here to bring something unique to make mankind better off because they contributed by showing the brightness of their star. We will help to build an alternative economy that is not built on greed and pollution, not built on nationality but on globalization.

If we can get every organization like the NAACP, black Baptist association, black lawyer association, black police association, black broadcasting association, on and on to make their current purchases of products and services from ELS we can create an 80 billion dollar industry overnight. We will give 90% profits back to the community or associations. Just to give an example, if the black Baptist association has 7 million members buying economically literate, a thousand dollars' worth of products and services through ELS, we charge the companies up to 10% for each transaction. This is what they spend on their advertisement budget anyway, and they pay us for bringing them an economically literate customer out of their advertisement budget, not expanding their budget, but at the same time enriching the community that has enriched their bottom line.

It is a symbiotic and principled collaboration in rebuilding a fair and just society. The black Baptist members buy their cell phones, their Internet, their car insurance, their mortgages just to amount to one thousand dollars in monthly bills. We put a pin # on your organization and you use that pin # on every transaction. We will get up to 10% on each transaction. If one thousand dollars is spent every month, that comes out to 100 dollars from each member. 7 million members' times 100 dollars create 700 million dollars each month for our communities. 25% will go to operation cost, out of that 25%, 20% will go to the sub-contractors who make the deals with the organization or an individual economically literate customer, 5% will go to ELS organizational structure.

The Dawn of The Age of Enlightenment

So out of that 700 million, 525 million will be profit, 90% of profit will go to the organization that partners with ELS. Our first ten years of partnership we will have generated in profit over 5.25 billion dollars of commerce for our communities, in which we now get nothing back.

No wonder we can't eliminate the ghettos and rural poverty and all the curses that comes with poverty. All ELS asks for is 10% from every partner to build life centers (new age schools) in the name of their organizations in every major city and surrounding rural areas.

No company will give away 90% of its profits like ELS, 90% of its profits that could be in the trillions of dollars. That is what true Kings and Queens do for their communities. No other companies will love you like ELS. There will be other companies that will copy our ideas and try to hurt our vision of rebuilding our inner cities and renewing opportunities in our rural areas and then from there on to the Caribbean Diaspora, into Latin America and then to Africa, and any impoverish people throughout the family of nations.

If one organization by only spending one thousand dollars with us can generate such massive profits, how much more could be if they spent every dollar economically literate. Imagine if our white brothers and sisters, Latino brothers and sisters, Asian brothers and sisters, Native American brothers and sisters, Muslim and Jewish brothers and sisters, all begin to buy through the ELS website globally, there would be nothing we can't solve in the economic realm. Then we will see each other as brothers and sisters from the same blood line traced by the DNA strand.

There would be nothing we can't solve in the sociological realm, for we are family, your mother and my mother are daughters of Eve, the DNA strand cannot lie, we are one family of nations.

AARP has 50 million members, if we get each member to become economically literate with one thousand dollars of their bill money, ELS get 10% of these transactions, (and by the way, what company wouldn't mind paying out their advertisement budget for 50 million new customers) that would be one hundred dollars per member we are generating out of this partnership. 100 dollars times 50 million members is 5 billion dollars per month we generate through economic literacy, 25% operation cost, we partner together 4 billion dollars a month that 48 billion dollars a year that our partnership has profited 10% goes to ELS. 56.2 billion dollars in AARP profit, by simply redirecting your members spending habits, where they get nothing back that significantly changes their lives. In 10 years that is 562 billion dollars you now have in your coffers to help every member with health care costs, with poverty issues, helping the less fortunate live lives of dignity and respect; elevating our senior citizens to the honor and respect they so richly deserves.

The Dawn of The Age of Enlightenment

We at ELS ask only 10% for life centers, (that we will build around the world that impoverished nations might become educated and equipped, that our companies like Walmart and Home Depot can begin to build in their nations, expanding their revenue streams and at the same time giving hopes of the American dream to every nation, what a legacy that America leaves, that she was truly the greatest nation in the history of man, not because of our fire power, but because of our power to love and treat others as we want to be treated). Imagine if every dollar was spent economically literate.

ELS will be creating millions of jobs. If a company puts their link to ELS website as a service provider or a product merchant (by the way it costs nothing to post your company on our website) they are investing in ELS. If we don't send you an economic literate customer, you pay us nothing, but if an economically literate buyer makes a transaction you pay out of your advertisement budget 10%. We don't make money unless you make money, which is principle centered leadership. If you make money, then the community is significantly benefited in a symbiotic relationship.

If the owner of that truck decides he wants to expand his business because he is getting overwhelmed by this new business coming in from ELS, he can diversify his company, by creating new revenue streams. For example, opening up a trucking school in the inner city or offering training and mentoring, creating clones of himself, teaching professionalism at the highest level of the trucking industry. He is creating a drug free working environment, not discriminating because of police records, and giving second chances, not with manual labor but teaching careers.

Imagine insurance companies, barber shops, brick masons, electricians, plumbers, car mechanics, engineers, Telecom companies and so on and on. Every trade, starting schools, cloning our successes, giving hope to school drop outs, cleaning our streets of drug dealer and the like because we are supporting our economically literate service and product providers. Our inner cities are like a plant, drained of its vitality because it lacked water. It lays over, about dead, but because of your goodwill you decided to water that flower even though it did not belong to you, when you returned later that day the plant was standing strong, because you watered it that morning, because you cared about it.

We at ELS propose to water the plant of our communities, we will water our communities with commerce and she will stand strong. We believe that if we work in a symbiotic partnership, we can rid our communities of the scourge of drugs, which leads to violence, jails and hell. ELS sends out a call to all drug dealers and others who live in darkness from knowledge and understanding, to come and be a part of this new world order, as our brothers and sisters.

The Dawn of The Age of Enlightenment

We want you to sell products from Walmart, Sears and every other company that posts on our website. After working for a good company, and paying your taxes, then you can buy a car, building your credit, in about a year or two you can buy a home, then you will be living the American dream. Not being destructive through the drug trade but being constructive by making every home economically literate and getting 20%, of that 10% we at ELS get from each economically literate customer.

Every ELS worker will urinate in a bottle for drug testing, from top to bottom. Every ELS employee will wear a shirt and tie and be clean cut, any drug test failure or violent incident will call for immediate termination. We will show that we are away from the scourge of drugs and violence. If as drug dealers they would go up interstates 95 and get off and make every community, crack infested, then I say we can go up and down every community and make every home economically literate. If there is approximately 80 to 90 billion dollars in the Latino community, 100's of billions of dollars in the white community, there will be lots of millionaires made through hard work and righteous living.

Wouldn't it be nice to see the scourge of drugs and violence and foul living gone from our inner cities and rural areas? When I was camping out in Virginia Beach, I was lying down in a camping tent, and there were hundreds of little caterpillars crawling around, a blue jay was hopping around eating and enjoying himself and enjoying life. I thought if God would plant a feast like that for a blue jay, how much more He wants the African American boys and girls in the ghettos, and Latino boys and girls in the barrios and all other boys and girls that are found in poverty to reach the maximum potential of their lives.

Every company from retail to wholesale, from gas stations to manufacturers posts on our website and becomes part of the ELS family, and it cost nothing, but by partnering with us we will bring in a new world order one transaction at a time. Every time I turn on the lights, I am helping rebuild the inner cities, every time I go on the Internet I am honoring the suffrage of the African people through this form of reparation that doesn't cost me anything but the self-discipline of how I spend my money, eliminating once and for all second class citizenship. This is what ELS was sent here to do; bringing the racial divide that breaks the heart of God, for Jesus said his disciples would be known by their love one for another. Every great religion teaches of brotherhood. ELS hopes to be the healing force of the universe, each nation planting a new seed of love and respect of one another, a world order where right is might not how much money you have. I call on every celebrity, every professional athlete, every minister, every man, every boy and every girl to stand up and take their rightful places as Kings and Queens, Princes and Princesses in the Kingdom of God. As eternal beings, let us now reach for our destiny, our very purpose for existing, to build one another up, to reach our unlimited potential as little gods.

The Dawn of The Age of Enlightenment

About The Author

Steve Alexander spent 32 years in the Telecom industry after graduating from the GTE-Sylvania Tech School, and has been active in Christian ministry for 28 years. His views on the plight of the American inner cities are shaped by over a decade's worth of experience teaching classes in the nation's prisons and working with inner city children in some of America's largest cities.

Steve is a family man, having been married to his wife Angela for 33 years, and has taught his three sons the value of hard work. One of his children is an FBI agent, and the other two work in the Telecom industry.

He is also a contributing author to the best seller "Million Man March Atonement", a moving spirit filled collaboration between the men who attended this remarkable gathering. Steve wrote about building a network based on his experiences running Alexander Telecom.

Steve is a visionary who believes he is called to rebuild our nation's inner cities, barrios, and Indian reservations. He feels God has called him to unify a divided nation, and a divided world.

Economic Leadership Solution

www.ingramcontent.com/pod-product-compliance
Lightning Source LLC
Chambersburg PA
CBHW050542280326
41933CB00011B/1688